# The ADHD Mom's Time Code

## A Guilt-Free System for Moms Who Lose Track of Time, Can't Stick to Schedules, and Are Done Feeling Like They're Failing

mf

# Disclaimer

By reading this guide, you are accepting the terms of this disclaimer in full. If you do not agree with these terms, please do not read or use this guide.

All content within this guide is provided for informational and educational purposes only and should not be considered medical, psychological, or other professional advice. The author is not a doctor, physician, psychologist, psychotherapist, counselor, or licensed healthcare provider. Reading or using this guide does not establish any form of a patient-client or therapeutic relationship.

Always consult with a physician, licensed therapist, or other qualified health professional regarding any questions or concerns you may have about your physical or mental health. Never disregard professional advice or delay seeking it because of something you have read in this guide.

The information presented in this guide is based on general research, personal interpretation, and publicly available sources. While reasonable efforts have been made to provide accurate and current information, the author and publisher make no representations or warranties about the completeness, accuracy, reliability, or suitability of the content. The author and publisher shall not be held liable for any errors, omissions, or outcomes related to the use of this guide.

You acknowledge that you are solely responsible for how you choose to use the information in this guide and that any actions you take based on this content are undertaken at your own risk. The publisher shall not be liable for any loss, injury, or damages arising from the application of any information provided herein.

This guide does not promise or guarantee any specific result, outcome, or improvement in well-being, mental health, or nervous system regulation. Individual results may vary.

Where applicable, any tools, concepts, or names mentioned are the property of their respective owners and are used strictly for identification or illustrative purposes. Their mention does not imply endorsement. Any individuals shown in the cover or promotional images are stock photography models, and image rights have been obtained through appropriate licensing agreements.

# Table of Contents

# Introduction

Every mother manages competing demands, but when you live with ADHD, juggling the needs of children, home, and work can feel uniquely overwhelming. For ADHD moms, keeping track of time is rarely straightforward.

Hours slip away, routines unravel quickly, and even the simplest plans may be derailed by unpredictable interruptions or moments of distraction. The result is often a day filled with half-finished tasks, forgotten commitments, and the uneasy feeling that you're always running behind no matter how hard you try.

Missing appointments or letting schedules slip can bring real challenges. Relationships with partners, children, and other caregivers can be strained by last-minute changes or chronic lateness. Opportunities at work or in your personal life may pass by because an event was missed or a form left unsigned at the bottom of a pile. Over time, these slips can build a persistent self-doubt and an internal voice whispering that you're disorganized, unreliable, or failing at the most basic expectations.

These experiences are not moral failings, but rather the practical effects of how ADHD influences your sense of time, memory, and planning. For many moms with ADHD, traditional time management advice simply doesn't fit daily reality. Rigorous schedules almost never persist, and complex planners can end up as clutter rather than solutions. This is not about lacking effort or discipline. Instead, ADHD can cause "time blindness," making it genuinely difficult to estimate how long things will take, anticipate bottlenecks, or recover from an interrupted flow.

Completing this guide gives you something quite different. Here, you'll encounter a curated set of practical, guilt-free tools designed specifically for the context of motherhood with ADHD. These strategies don't require perfection or rigid systems; they provide flexible ways to observe your real patterns, create manageable routines, and respond kindly to setbacks. You'll find support for regaining a sense of control over your day, learning to adjust on the fly, and showing yourself greater kindness each step of the way.

This resource focuses on everyday household and family experiences rather than formal clinical diagnosis, medication, or work-based accommodations. Instead, it zeroes in on the practical pain points of home life: mornings with kids, meal planning, school forms, fluctuating work demands, and the thousand microtransitions that fill each day. The guidance here is designed with your actual priorities and environment in mind.

***In this guide, you will learn:***

- Why ADHD affects time management so deeply for mothers in multitasking roles
- How to map your personal daily patterns and identify where time most often escapes
- Strategies for building flexible routines and "scheduling without schedules"
- Tools for supporting memory and externalizing important reminders in ADHD-friendly ways

- Low-pressure accountability systems that encourage gentle follow-through instead of harsh policing
- Exercises and tools for nurturing self-acceptance, even when time slips happen

Each chapter focuses on a different layer of the ADHD mom's time experience, building towards a system that is adaptable, compassionate, and practical. You won't find one-size-fits-all solutions. Instead, you'll gain building blocks to create your own "time code" , a way of honoring your strengths, supporting your specific challenges, and building a foundation for days that feel more possible.

If you have wondered why time feels so slippery or why conventional advice doesn't stick, you are not alone. The next chapters will help you understand your unique experience of time and begin the process of shaping a system that finally works for you.

# Understanding ADHD Time Blindness in Motherhood

Motherhood expects you to be everywhere at once: caring for a child, managing housework, handling logistics, and often juggling a job too. For moms with ADHD, time seems especially slippery. The day can feel chaotic before breakfast is over, and every effort to "get back on track" can dissolve before you even know you need to. This chapter opens up the heart of that struggle: ADHD time blindness in motherhood, what it looks like, how it feels, and how to begin seeing its patterns.

Unlike the struggles of ordinary distraction or forgetfulness, time blindness eats away at hours, making it honestly difficult to measure, allocate, or even notice the passage of time. Let's take a closer look at how this phenomenon crops up for moms who are constantly multitasking.

## Core Symptoms of Time Blindness in ADHD Moms

Time blindness is not just about running late; it's a persistent mismatch between plans and realities. For moms with ADHD, core symptoms show up in deeply practical ways:

- Losing track of whole hours while "just finishing up" one small task.
- Immersing so deeply in a single activity (scrolling, cleaning, answering emails) that other responsibilities are forgotten.

- Intending to start morning routines early, only to look up and realize it's already time to leave.
- Overestimating how much can fit into a given block—optimistically thinking, "I'll just do one more thing," and missing windows for leaving, meals, or transitions.
- Underestimating or overlooking "hidden" time drains like getting shoes on kids, finding backpacks, or handling a meltdown in the car.
- Chronic lateness or unpredictable early/late arrivals, regardless of reminders or repeated efforts.

The result is not an occasional oversight but a recurring struggle that undermines self-trust and makes "keeping up" feel impossible. Even days that begin with a solid plan can leave a mom feeling that hours simply disappeared.

Next, to untangle these overwhelming experiences, a structured approach helps bring hidden patterns into focus.

## The "Lost Hours" Framework: Pinpointing Where Time Escapes

Every mom with ADHD feels the sensation of a day vanishing, but rarely is there a clear sense of where the time actually went. This is the value of the "Lost Hours" framework: a practice for identifying daily time black holes and pinpointing exactly which activities and transitions tend to swallow the most minutes.

***To use the "Lost Hours" framework, take these steps:***

1. Choose a typical day (not the most chaotic, not the smoothest).
2. Mentally divide the day into clear segments: morning prep, school drop-off, work or home management, midday routines, afternoon transitions, evening.
3. At the end of each segment or as soon as possible ask yourself: "When did I last notice the time? What was I doing right before I felt 'lost'?"
4. Make a quick note (phone or notepad): jot down the exact activity or interruption that preceded the black hole (e.g., "misplaced car keys," "lost track on Instagram," "child needed a snack").
5. At day's end, review your notes to spot patterns. Are there activities, times of day, or types of interruptions that seem to appear most often?

Through this process, many moms find that the same triggers keep recurring. The black holes are rarely random. Instead, they concentrate around certain routines, tasks that lack a defined endpoint, or sequences disrupted by unexpected needs from children. Naming these "lost hours" gives a real starting point for smarter adjustments, rather than vague self-blame.

## Identifying High-Risk Moments: Transitions and Child-Care Interruptions

For ADHD moms, time loss spikes during transitions, those moments when you need to switch gears, go from one role to another, or respond to a sudden need. These switch points are naturally vulnerable, but ADHD magnifies their unpredictability.

***Some high-risk transition moments include:***

- Moving from personal time to parenting tasks (e.g., wrapping up an email as a toddler calls from another room)
- Leaving the house with kids (gathering snacks, shoes, supplies always takes longer than expected)
- Switching between work-at-home tasks and hands-on child care (even brief interruptions can derail focus for the rest of the hour)
- Transitioning into family meals or bedtime routines (everyone is tired, and interruptions easily cascade)
- Returning to a previously paused task after a child's interruption (it takes extra time to remember what you were doing and why)

During these transitions, ADHD may cause difficulty disengaging from one task or shifting attention fully to what's next. The mind resists switching, and kids' needs interrupt at unpredictable intervals, making it easy to lose time and sequence. Recognizing these high-risk junctures creates a map for where buffer time or external reminders could make the most difference.

## Checklist: ADHD-Driven Time Errors or Typical Parental Forgetfulness?

Ordinary forgetfulness is common for all parents, given constant demands and fatigue. However, ADHD brings unique challenges that go beyond the usual interpersonal chaos of family life. Use this checklist to distinguish ADHD-driven time issues from everyday absentmindedness:

***ADHD-Driven Time Errors:***

- Regularly unable to judge how long a task will really take (washing dishes, putting kids to bed, getting out the door)
- Losing track of time when not externally cued (no timers, no alarms, no immediate deadlines)
- Hyperfocusing on one activity to the exclusion of all else—only stopping when interrupted
- Consistent challenges with starting transitions on time, even with intention and reminders
- Forgetting time-sensitive tasks despite having reminders or notes in plain sight (not just "missed" but "mentally filtered out")
- Repeating the same timing mistakes daily or weekly, despite feedback or extra effort to improve

***Typical Parental Forgetfulness:***

- Lateness or missed tasks only during periods of high stress, sleep deprivation, or illness
- Can generally self-correct with a reminder or short-term effort (e.g., "set a phone alarm" works as intended)
- Occasional memory lapses, but patterns vary rather than repeating predictably
- Able to finish most tasks in planned time blocks if children are occupied or routines are followed
- "Forgetting" mainly when overloaded or when multitasking is pushed to extremes

If most of your experiences align with the ADHD column, it is likely that time blindness is playing a central role in your challenges. If they cluster in the ordinary column, typical life stressors may be a bigger factor than ADHD.

This distinction is vital for self-understanding and for advocating for appropriate support rather than feeling guilty or "broken."

The next section addresses a frequent secondary struggle: others often misunderstand, mislabel, or minimize ADHD-driven difficulties with time, especially when observed from outside the family.

## Common External Misunderstandings and the Challenge of Explaining ADHD Time Blindness

Many people, including partners, grandparents, and even children, assume lateness or disorganization must be a sign of carelessness or lack of effort. For moms, this outside skepticism can feel especially punishing, adding misunderstanding to the internal frustration of time blindness.

***Some common external misunderstandings include:***

- Assuming that reminders or scolding will "fix" missed timings ("Just use your phone/calendar, it's not hard").
- Framing lateness as intentionally disrespectful rather than neurologically driven ("You just don't care about being on time").

- Underestimating the invisible work it takes to manage shifting family needs ("It's the same routine every day, how is it always chaos?").
- Believing that "trying harder" or adding more effort will translate directly into change.
- Comparing with non-ADHD parents who thrive on strict routines, further isolating the ADHD mom.

These misinterpretations can create new stress and make it even harder for moms to seek help or advocate for accommodations. Effective communication using neutral, informed language can bridge the gap. That's where a language sheet becomes a practical tool.

## Language Sheet: Ways to Explain Time Blindness to Partners and Kids

When explaining ADHD-driven time struggles, using clear scripts helps reduce defensiveness and builds understanding. Below is a language sheet to guide conversations.

***For Partners/Co-Parents:***

- "Sometimes I honestly don't feel time passing the way you do. I can finish just one thing, and then a whole hour is gone without me realizing."
- "It isn't that I don't care about schedules, it's that my brain loses track more quickly, especially when I'm switching roles or handling interruptions."

- “Reminders help, but they don’t always cut through if I’m super focused or stressed. I need systems that check in with me, not just alarms I can swipe away.”
- “If you notice I’m drifting off-timeline, please gently redirect me instead of getting frustrated. I’m working on it, and sometimes outside cues help a lot.”

***For Kids (age-appropriate):***

- “Sometimes Mom gets so focused on one thing that she forgets what time it is. If you see me taking too long, you can say, ‘Hey Mom, is it time to go?’”
- “I might ask you for reminders about snacks, meals, or bedtime because my brain sometimes skips ahead or gets stuck.”
- “Everyone’s brain keeps time a little differently. Mine needs extra help from tools and from you.”

Neutral, honest language takes blame out of the equation while acknowledging real challenges. It also invites family members to participate in supportive, practical ways rather than policing or shaming.

To summarize, ADHD moms face time blindness as a daily impediment to managing multiple roles. Understanding the symptoms, using a structured approach to map “lost hours,” and recognizing high-risk transitions begins to break the cycle of confusion and guilt. Distinguishing ADHD-driven errors from ordinary forgetfulness is foundational, and having ready scripts for external communication fosters the understanding and support needed to try new tools.

In the next chapter, the lens will shift from recognition to action: exploring why ADHD creates a nonlinear experience of time, and how to visualize, map, and work with those pulses rather than fighting against them. This deeper insight will provide the groundwork for building systems that adapt to your real-life cadence without requiring rigid adherence to schedules that were never built for ADHD minds or for the fast-moving world of motherhood.

# The Nonlinear Day: Embracing the Reality of ADHD Time Flow

The rhythm of ADHD in motherhood is rarely linear. Instead, it runs in unpredictable surges and dips, shaped by fluctuating energy, varying focus, and shifts in motivation that defy any traditional schedule. Where the earlier discussion examined how time blindness complicates daily life for moms, this chapter dives into a new lens: how to see and work with the actual patterns of an ADHD day, rather than constantly battling them. Understanding the true flow of a nonlinear day is a pivotal step in moving from perpetual self-correction to proactive, self-compassionate planning.

Every ADHD mom has likely experienced the mismatch between what she meant to accomplish and what actually happened. Not all hours are created equal, some slide by without notice, some are packed with effort yet yield little, and others deliver surprising bursts of productivity. The concept of the nonlinear day is about recognizing, mapping, and eventually leveraging those underlying waves, instead of being caught off-guard by them.

## Mapping the "ADHD Pulse": Charting Energy, Focus, and Motivation

Central to managing time with ADHD is learning to see one's day and week not as a smooth, clock-driven landscape, but as a series of pulses. These pulses reflect natural peaks and valleys in energy, focus, and motivation that can look and feel completely out of step with outside expectations. Recognizing these rhythms allows for smarter, more forgiving routines.

***For ADHD moms, these fluctuations might look like:***

- Sudden morning energy that dissipates by late morning, making complex tasks easier before 10am but nearly impossible by noon.
- An unpredictable "second wind" after dinner, where motivation for chores or planning returns even as everyone else winds down.
- Afternoon slumps where brain fog sets in, signals are missed, or every request feels harder to process.
- Motivation spikes linked to novelty such as renewed bursts of energy for a new project, shifting quickly to boredom or overwhelm when novelty fades.

To get a handle on these patterns, consider charting them over a week. Take a notebook or use a phone app, and briefly rate (1–5) your energy, focus, and motivation at a few set times each day morning, midday, mid-afternoon, and evening. After several days, some trends are likely to emerge: consistent low-energy zones, reliable high-focus windows, recurring slumps.

By visually tracking these waves, ADHD moms no longer need to wonder if their experience is random or "just them." The goal is not perfection but increased clarity which can form the basis for making real, sustainable changes to routines, rather than simply hoping each day will be different.

Next, one must deal with the daily reality of invisible labor: the small, never-ending tasks that quietly eat up time and mental bandwidth.

## Tabulation Tool for Logging Invisible Labor and Micro-Tasks

A significant challenge for ADHD moms involves invisible labor. Every day is filled with a multitude of micro-tasks, small, often overlooked actions that are necessary to keep life running but rarely make it onto any list. Logging these can help reveal sources of attention fragmentation and hidden time drains.

Use the following table as a daily logging template for a week. Track each micro-task or act of invisible labor as you notice it, grouping activities by type or time of day if useful.

***Invisible Labor & Micro-Task Log***

| Time | Task Description | Duration (min) | Distraction/ Interruption Source |
|---|---|---|---|
| 7:15 am | Searching for clean socks | 5 | Child request |
| 10:30 am | Emailing teacher | 8 | Reminder pop-up |
| 12:10 pm | Cleaning up spilled snack | 3 | Child accident |
| 1:40 pm | Refilling medication sorter | 4 | Phone notification |
| 4:00 pm | Sorting mail | 7 | Lost focus, opened social media |
| 7:25 pm | Setting up school backpack | 6 | TV distraction |

As this kind of record grows, patterns stand out. Which types of tasks consume the most time? Do certain distractions or interruptions cluster around specific times? Are some invisible tasks repeated daily but always skipped in planning?

This tabulation serves two goals: making invisible work visible, and helping prioritize or automate recurring micro-tasks whenever possible. Over time, this awareness enables adjustment either by condensing or delegating routine tasks or by planning "fragment slots" to accommodate the inevitable flow of micro-tasks.

Attention often fails as these small disruptions accumulate. Anticipating the signals of drifting attention can provide an early warning, steering things back on course before a commitment is completely missed.

## Rule Set: Early Indicators of Drifting Attention

Reliable routines begin with recognizing the specific signs that focus is starting to slip. Spotting early indicators allows for faster, gentler course correction, reducing the risk that minor lapses lead to major missed commitments or lost hours.

***Key rules for noticing drifting attention include:***

1. **Physical restlessness:** Fidgeting, foot tapping, or frequently shifting position when previously settled.
2. **Task flipping:** Repeatedly moving between unrelated activities (e.g., pausing laundry mid-load to answer a text, then starting dinner, then forgetting both).
3. **Sudden forgetfulness:** Realizing a train of thought is gone or no longer remembering what was just about to be done.
4. **Increased sensitivity:** Becoming easily annoyed or frustrated by interruptions, noise, or requests.

5. **Loss of time cues:** Looking up and realizing much more time has passed than intended, often paired with hyperfocus or total zoning out.

***When two or more of these indicators present themselves, it is time to pause. Rather than pressing on or berating oneself, try one of these stopgap actions:***

- Stand and stretch, or move briefly to a new location.
- Check the external environment: is a reminder, timer, or visual cue needed now?
- Take a short self-check break: name the last three things accomplished, then state the next one intended task aloud or in writing.
- Reduce stimuli: silence unnecessary notifications, step away from noisy spaces, or put on headphones.

By treating drifting attention as a cue not a failure the ADHD mom can prevent smaller slips from snowballing into forgotten appointments, burnt dinners, or prolonged tangles of unfinished tasks.

A visual sense of the day's unique rhythm further grounds these concepts in practical reality.

## Visual Sample Timeline: The Non-Typical ADHD Motherhood Day

Illustrating a day in the life of an ADHD mom makes the nonlinear cadence immediately visual. This timeline maps fluctuating energy, frequent micro-tasks, transition disruptions, and the persistence of invisible labor. Consider the following representation:

***Sample ADHD Mom Nonlinear Day Timeline***

| Time | Focus/Energy | Main Activity | Micro-Tasks / Distractions |
|---|---|---|---|
| 6:45 am | High | School prep | Hunt for shoes, unexpected tantrum |
| 8:30 am | Moderate | Drop-off, start work/chores | Email distraction, coffee spill |
| 10:00 am | Low | Work block interrupted | Phone call, snack demand, laundry check |
| 12:30 pm | Slump | Kid lunch, errands | Deep fatigue, forget return call |
| 2:45 pm | Slight rise | Afternoon reset | Dishes, social scroll breaks in tasks |
| 4:15 pm | Medium | Homework help, dinner prep | Arguing siblings, missing ingredients |
| 6:00 pm | Upturn | Family time, cleaning | Mismatch in routines, lost time hunting socks |
| 8:30 pm | Varies | Kids to bed, planning next day | Clutter overwhelm, forgotten chore |
| 9:30 pm | Late energy | Creative or focused burst | Late-night "catch-up" spiral |

***This illustration highlights several truths of the nonlinear ADHD day in motherhood:***

- Peak attention often coincides with high-demand periods, creating strain.
- Slumps and surges are predictable but not on a standard schedule.
- Breakdown points cluster around transitions and when micro-tasks pile up.
- Inattention and fatigue compound in the afternoon, making impulse control and memory more fragile.

Revisiting these visual timelines over several weeks can clarify where intervention makes the most difference between anchor points for consistent routines, optimized windows for intense focus, and buffer slots to absorb delays without guilt.

The nonlinear pattern, however, brings a risk: what starts as flexible adaptation sometimes tips into chaos. Recognizing warning flags is the next step in staying out of time spirals.

## Warning Flags: When Nonlinear Routines Slide Into Chaos

While flexibility is the core strength of the nonlinear day, warning flags emerge when routines collapse and spiraling problems set in. Awareness and timely action are crucial to prevent full-blown overwhelm.

***Common warning flags include:***

- Missing or skipping "must-do" routines repeatedly (meals, medication, school pick-ups).
- Pervasive sense of chasing tasks all day but finishing few.
- Multiple days of waking up anxious about what was left undone.

- Growing frustration or irritability toward family members, often rooted in compounded time slips.
- Home or work spaces showing escalating clutter tasks begun but not completed, supplies or belongings left out.
- Abandonment of previously helpful supports or reminders, often replaced by avoidance or self-criticism.

***If two or more warning flags appear, try these stopgap actions:***

- Pause and inventory: List the absolute essentials for the next block (the true "musts," not "shoulds").
- Enlist help, temporarily delegate, or skip noncritical tasks.
- Use a single, large visual cue (sticky note, reminder board) to triage next actions, blocking out major distractions for 15–30 minutes.
- Announce a "reset" aloud to children or partners if possible, signaling a shift rather than piling on more self-pressure.

These stopgaps are not about perfection or catching up on everything. They serve to prevent slipping further into chaos and to re-anchor the day in manageable priorities. Over time, the ability to spot these warning flags early can reduce frustration and preserve self-kindness—the core mission of the ADHD Mom's Time Code.

Living with ADHD does not mean resigning to disorder. Instead, it asks for a more honest map—one that respects the real pulses, demands, and adaptive strengths of an ADHD mind negotiating motherhood. Harnessing the nonlinear rhythm, logging invisible labor, spotting drift early, visualizing the true shape of a day, and acting on warning flags: these are the practical essentials that lay the groundwork for guilt-free, flexible time systems designed for ADHD, not perfectionism.

This orientation toward self-mapping and gentle adjustment, rather than strict scheduling, forms the foundation for the next set of tools. The following chapter will translate this understanding into practical steps for conducting a time audit rooted not in blame, but in generous noticing and small, possible changes.

# The Guilt-Free Time Audit

Shifting from the previous chapter's honest portrayal of nonlinear days, this chapter steps into practical territory. Rather than simply observing the patterns of fluctuating attention and invisible labor, the focus now moves to an active, guilt-free way to make sense of where time "goes."

For moms with ADHD, recording time loss can easily invite harsh self-judgment or a sense of failure. The Guilt-Free Time Audit changes that narrative by centering curiosity and self-kindness. Here, time slips, wins, and interruptions are tracked with neutral noticing, not blame.

## Stepwise Process for Conducting a Self-Kind Time Accounting

The heart of the Guilt-Free Time Audit lies in its gentle, stepwise approach. Unlike traditional productivity methods, which often push for efficiency at the cost of compassion, this time audit invites honest tracking with no assumption that "perfection" is possible or even desirable within ADHD motherhood.

1. **Start with a Neutral Mindset**. Begin each audit period (day or half-day slots work best) with a brief pause. Remind yourself the goal is awareness, not "catching mistakes." This attitude sets the tone for noticing, not judging.
2. **Choose a Simple Tracking Tool.** This can be a notebook, a printable template, or even voice notes if writing feels

cumbersome. Keep it accessible to avoid friction when logging entries.

3. **Log Time as it Actually Flows.** Instead of planning in advance, jot down entries as things unfold. Focus on moments when time "slips" (unexpected delays, forgotten tasks), as well as times of smooth flow or positive surprises.
4. **Mark Disruptions and Context.** When noticing a disruption, briefly note what happened: Was it a child's interruption, a phone alert, or waning motivation? This builds understanding of vulnerability points without blame.
5. **Notice and Celebrate Positive Exceptions.** If a task takes less time than expected or is completed despite distractions, record it. These moments are data points worth honoring, not dismissing.
6. **Review with Curiosity.** At regular intervals (end of day or after a rough patch), look over the entries. Ask questions like, "Where did my time actually go?" or "What factors helped or hindered me?" Skip any self-criticism, imagine you are studying a weather pattern, not reviewing a test.

This process allows for a self-kind audit that honors the realities of ADHD time flow. Instead of reinforcing old cycles of guilt, it offers new perspective and actionable visibility.

## Audit Template for Tracking Time Slippages, Positive Exceptions, and Unavoidable Disruptions

Having a concrete template makes it easier to capture the nuances of an ADHD mom's day. This audit is designed for minimal overhead and maximum compassion, with space to note both struggles and unexpected successes.

*Guilt-Free Time Audit Template:*

**Column 1: Time/Task**

- What were you trying to do?
- Time you started (roughly)

**Column 2: Actual Outcome**

- Did you finish, get interrupted, or run late?
- Brief result (done, paused, delayed, skipped)

**Column 3: Interruption/Slip Details**

- What caused the slip (internal distraction, child, external phone call, fatigue, etc.)?
- Was it avoidable or genuinely out of your control?

**Column 4: Feelings/Thoughts**

- How did you feel in the moment (frustrated, relieved, resigned, proud)?
- Anything you want to remember for next time

**Column 5: Positive Exceptions**

- Record any tasks that went smoother or faster than usual

- Note any improvisations or creative pivots

By maintaining this template over several days, patterns emerge: are there consistent times or contexts where interruptions spike? Are there hidden strengths or adaptations? The data collected in this way becomes a foundation for refining routines, requesting support, or simply validating the true nature of daily demands.

Moving forward, it becomes crucial to differentiate between what is actually necessary within the home and internal sphere, versus what comes from the persistent, sometimes unrealistic, expectations of others.

## Practices for Separating External Expectations from Internal Priorities

Many sources of time-driven guilt arise not from genuine personal priorities, but from pressure to meet the standards of schools, workplaces, or extended families. For ADHD moms, the difference between "what must get done" and "what others say should be done" is often blurry, feeding constant comparison and frustration. These practices help create that needed separation.

- **Identify Non-Negotiables.** List all routines and commitments that are truly required; these are tasks with unavoidable consequences if missed, such as school pickups or essential work calls.
- **List External Pressures.** Write down expectations regularly voiced by others: comments from teachers, relatives, work, online groups, or well-meant advice from friends.

- **Compare and Question.** For each external expectation, ask: Is this urgent for my family's actual functioning? Or is it someone else's version of "should"?
- **Affirm Internal Priorities.** Make a shorter list of what actually improves daily life or well-being. This includes both essential tasks and self-care "needs," however small.
- **Adjust the Time Audit Lens.** When reviewing daily entries, specifically label which tasks came from outside expectations, and which were personally meaningful. Over time, shift more focus and praise toward tasks that reflect internal priorities.

By consciously drawing this line, moms learn to invest energy where it matters most, rather than scattering effort across unwanted, externally imposed "shoulds." This not only clarifies workload, but can also relieve the chronic guilt of failing to "do it all."

At this juncture, it is natural for guilt triggers to emerge when reviewing time slips or missed obligations. The next section offers a structured way to recognize and compassionately reframe them.

## Table of Common Guilt Triggers and ADHD-Aware Reframes

Many moms with ADHD share a set of recurring guilt triggers tied closely to cultural or community expectations. By naming these triggers and pairing them with conscious reframes, it becomes possible to interrupt the cycle of self-blame.

*Common Guilt Triggers Table:*

| Guilt Trigger | ADHD-Aware Reframe |
|---|---|
| "I missed another school deadline." | "Deadlines challenge my time-awareness. Systems can help, and missing one doesn't make me neglectful." |
| "I forgot a friend's birthday call." | "My attention slips aren't proof of not caring. Genuine relationships withstand the quirks of ADHD." |
| "Another dinner started late." | "Late dinners are part of our family rhythm. Nourishing my family matters more than precise timing." |
| "I took longer to recover after an interruption." | "Transitioning back is harder with ADHD. Recognizing this is a sign of awareness—not failure." |
| "Tasks pile up because I lose track of small things." | "Invisible labor adds up fast. Listing what got done shows the reality behind the scenes." |
| "I needed to rest instead of finish chores." | "Rest is a valid choice when focus is depleted. Productivity isn't always the best measure of value." |

Reading through this table during or after a time audit enables ADHD moms to replace punitive thoughts with self-compassionate ones. It also builds resilience for when guilt surfaces in the future.

To reinforce self-forgiveness, one last practical tool is offered: written or visual "permission slips" for when tasks, presence, or timing fall short of what others (or previous self-standards) expect.

## "Permission Slips" Card Set for Absences, Delays, and Skipped Tasks Without Self-Blame

The "permission slip" is a simple but powerful exercise. Contrary to the critical internal monologue that arises with each delay or lost item, these slips serve as reminders that lapses can be accepted, not punished. Here is a practical set designed for quick reference. Moms may write these on sticky notes, phone screens, or index cards for use as needed.

***Sample Permission Slips:***

- "It's allowed to be late when the morning falls apart. My presence matters more than my promptness."
- "Skipping today's laundry doesn't make me a failure. It makes me a human living with ADHD."
- "I have permission to say 'no' to extra requests when my mental load is already full."
- "It's okay to ask for help or drop a non-essential chore. This protects my energy for what it means most."
- "Resting or recharging is not a waste of time. It is necessary for my well-being, and that matters."

Moms can personalize these slips or invent their own. The key is to create a physical cue—a written proof—to intercept the habitual guilt reaction and remind oneself that flexibility is not only allowed but needed within the ADHD Time Code.

The Guilt-Free Time Audit aims not just to track time, but to transform the emotional relationship ADHD moms have with their daily rhythms. By moving from critical self-surveillance toward neutral, curious noticing, the audit exposes both the reality of time slippages and the legitimacy of invisible effort. A structured template helps capture all aspects of lived time—losses, exceptions, and genuinely uncontrollable events—so that days are evaluated with honesty, not harshness.

The separation of true internal priorities from inherited external expectations reduces the mental clutter that breeds resentment and burnout. Naming and reframing guilt, with the support of practical permission slips, fortifies a cycle of self-compassion rather than endless criticism. These strategies not only make future audits easier, but also set the stage for the next layer of the ADHD Mom's Time Code: creating daily structure that honors the unpredictable while building more supportive and workable routines.

If the audit process raises distress or causes persistent negative emotions, revisit the safety note in the earlier chapter and consider consulting with a qualified support professional.

# The "Time Code" Framework for Scheduling Without Schedules

Moving forward, the previous chapter established a mindset of curious observation and self-kindness in tracking time. Building on that foundation, it now becomes possible to craft daily rhythms with a system that does not punish unpredictability, but instead adapts to it. For moms with ADHD, the drive is not toward rigid perfection but toward making life manageable and less stressful, especially when countless moving pieces can derail even the best intentions.

Traditional scheduling methods, with their strict blocks of time and precise start and end points, often set up ADHD moms for disappointment. The ADHD Mom's Time Code offers a different way: a structure that flexes with the very real unpredictability of motherhood and the rhythms of an ADHD mind. The purpose of this chapter is to introduce a framework that organizes days without depending on the concept of unwavering schedules.

## The Color Block System: Creating Needs-Based Routines

The core of the "Time Code" Framework is the Color Block System. Instead of mapping out rigid hourly plans, this system groups types of activities into colored segments, each representing a broad category of need or focus. For example, blue might stand for "rest and recharge," green for "household tasks," orange for "kid time," and so on.

This approach aligns expectations with real needs rather than arbitrary timelines. Instead of planning "from 12:00 to 12:30 is lunch," a mom creates a visual representation showing that between the end of the morning and a non-negotiable event like school pick-up, the "green" block stands for chores and the "blue" block signals a break. The colors signal intent and allow for shifting durations depending on what unfolds.

***Implementation steps for the Color Block System:***

- List core need categories for the day (such as meals, work, rest, child care, errands, play).
- Assign a unique color to each category, using markers, colored pencils, or digital tools.
- Draw a simple, horizontal band or segmented wheel for the day, using colored segments to represent periods for those activity types, not precise times.
- Allow the length of each colored zone to reflect priority or expected energy—longer for frequent or draining needs, shorter for quick tasks or things that cannot always be controlled.
- Post the chart somewhere easily seen (fridge, family whiteboard, planner), so both predictability and flexibility are visible.

This visual anchor provides an immediate, forgiving sense of structure that is not undone by unexpected events. If a meal takes longer or a child needs extra attention, the blocks may adjust without creating a ripple of guilt across the rest of the day.

Transitioning from core routine mapping, the next focus is on making room for the truly non-negotiable portions of daily life.

## Customizable Anchor Points for Non-Negotiable Events

While most of the day can remain fluid, certain moments—like school drop-offs and work meetings—are non-negotiable and have real consequences if missed. Rather than locking every surrounding minute into a strict sequence, the Time Code system creates customizable anchor points.

***Key characteristics of effective anchor points:***

- Clearly defined (e.g., "School pick-up at 2:45 PM" or "Zoom call at 10:00 AM").
- Marked on the color block chart with a strong border, sticker, or bolded text.
- Surrounded by flexible buffer blocks of time to allow for transitions, preparation, or recovery (see next chapter for more on buffer zones).

***How to integrate anchor points:***

- Identify next day's must-do fixed events.
- Mark these anchor points on a chart before filling in flexible color blocks.
- Plan around each anchor by allowing flexible activities to "float" up to, but not past, these set spots.
- Avoid packing activities so tightly before or after anchors that transitions become stressful.

By prioritizing anchor points and cushioning them with buffer blocks (often represented by a neutral or 'white' strip on the chart), the day becomes both structured for what must happen and Permissive for what can shift.

With anchors in place, attention can shift to the flexible elements that dominate much of an ADHD-influenced day.

## Flexible Time Buckets: Chores, Play, Rest, and Contingency

Most daily tasks for ADHD moms do not require minute-by-minute accounting. Instead, dividing the day into broad time buckets each matched to a color block creates space for responsiveness rather than constant rescheduling.

***Time buckets are intentionally flexible categories. The recommendations below support this approach:***

- **Chores:** Group together tasks like dishes, laundry, and tidying into a distinct bucket (color green, for example). This bucket floats between anchors based on daily energy and interruptions.
- **Play/Kid Time:** Designate a color (such as orange) to signal active play, reading, or outings. Let this bucket expand if kids need more attention or contract when independent play is possible.
- **Rest/Recharge:** Assign blue or another calming color to nap time, solo reading, or mental reset periods. Encourage use even if the "rest" moment is short.
- **Contingency/Buffer:** Reserve an unassigned or neutral-colored block for spillover, last-minute needs, or stress recovery. Placing

contingency periods strategically creates a pressure release for days that run late or fall apart.

***A sample prioritization:***

- If a child becomes sick, the “play” bucket may merge with “rest” or “contingency,” while chores can wait for a later opening.
- If there is a burst of energy, chore and project buckets can be pursued more intensively, with permission to shrink them again as focus wanes.

By relying on buckets rather than fixed time slots, moms are empowered to respond to their actual environment instead of chasing a failing timetable. Taking the above elements together, seeing it all in practice can help clarify how to set up an initial daily chart.

## Example Layout: The “Time Code” Daily Chart

A practical chart translates the Color Block System, anchor points, and time buckets into a visible, customizable daily tool. The following example offers a functional layout for quick setup and ongoing adjustment.

***Sample “Time Code” Daily Chart:***

| Time Range | Color/ Block | Activity or Need | Anchor Point? | Notes/ Comments |
|---|---|---|---|---|
| 7:00–8:00 AM | Yellow | Wake-up/ Breakfast | No | Transition time is flexible |
| 8:00–9:30 AM | Green | Chores/ Errands | No | Pause as needed |
| 9:30–10:00 AM | Red Border | Work Call | Yes | Anchor: must start 10:00 |

| 10:00–12:00 PM | Orange | Kid Play/ Activities | No | Can slide forward/back |
|---|---|---|---|---|
| 12:00–12:30 PM | Blue | Rest/Break | No | Add quick rest if running late |
| 12:30–2:15 PM | Green | Project/Household Tasks | No | Move to play if needed |
| 2:15–2:45 PM | Red Border | School Pick-Up | Yes | Anchor, non-negotiable |
| 2:45–4:00 PM | Orange | Kid Time/ Outdoor Play | No | Shift duration as needed |
| 4:00–5:30 PM | Gray | Contingency/ Free Block | No | Use for spillovers/ missed tasks |
| 5:30–6:30 PM | Yellow | Dinner/ Family Wind-Down | No | Flexible, decompress together |

***How this chart works:***

- Colored bands replace exact times with zones and intentions.
- Anchor points (like work calls and school pick-ups) get a stand-out border or notation.
- Day can be updated by simply redrawing, erasing, or adjusting blocks in response to unexpected changes.
- Free or contingency blocks absorb time slippages and give psychological space.

Adapt this chart with preferred colors, needs, or sequence. Visual cues are the primary tool for recall and time awareness, not alarms or notifications that may add stress. Now, the real world brings its own challenges, and even the best-laid blocks can slip or overlap. Addressing these moments directly is key to sustained use.

## Troubleshooting Guide: When Time Blocks Slip or Overlap

Consistently missing or over-extending time blocks is not a sign of failure; it signals the need for adjustment. This troubleshooting guide offers targeted solutions for common issues that arise with the Time Code system.

*Common Issues and Solutions:*

1. **Time Blocks Always Run Over**
    - Shorten the block's expected activity list. Use smaller increments or cut out low-priority tasks.
    - Add larger or more frequent contingency blocks.
    - Notice if transition needs (shifting from one activity to the next) are underestimated. Extend buffer time.

2. **Anchor Points Are Frequently Missed or Approached in a Rush**
    - Place a physical reminder or use a timer for just the anchor, not the whole block.
    - Place buffer/rest blocks prior to anchors to create a clear, low-pressure lead-in.
    - Re-examine preceding blocks and trim their scope to prevent overrun.

3. **Certain Blocks Regularly Get Skipped**
    - Test moving or reordering the block perhaps energy is too low at that time.

- Pair skipped activities with something enjoyable or essential ("Have snack during chores").
- As needed, shrink the block into "microtime" units (e.g., five minutes of a task, not thirty).

4. **Overlapping Needs (Multiple Kids, Competing Demands)**
   - Color-code responsibilities for multiple people (Mom's time vs. kid time) on the same chart.
   - If tasks continuously collide, rework blocks to be sequential rather than parallel.

5. **Overwhelm Due to Chart Complexity**
   - Reduce the number of colors or categories, focusing only on the highest-need routines.
   - Use a simple "AM/PM" system before layering additional details.

Failure does not come from shifting a block; it emerges only if self-critique prevents adaptation. Each daily adjustment is valid data and an act of self-preservation.

For situations where persistent stress, anxiety, or deeper struggles are attached to daily planning or frequent disruptions, revisit the safety note in the earlier chapter and consider professional support.

By treating the day as a living system rather than a train on a track, ADHD moms gain room to breathe and rebuild a sense of capacity. The "Time Code" framework, with its color blocks, anchor points, flexible buckets, customizable charts, and troubleshooting methods, forms a toolkit designed for real life. It supports not only the varied demands of modern motherhood but also the unique, nonlinear relationship with time that defines the ADHD experience.

The next stage brings in external supports—physical, digital, and sensory aids to extend memory and focus, so the systems created today are remembered and sustained as circumstances evolve.

# Externalizing Memory and Managing Distractions

Shifting from color-coded Time Code charts and the freedom of flexible anchors, many mothers with ADHD find that even the best visual routines can unravel when memory lapses or surprise distractions take over. The next logical focus is not to perfect the Time Code framework, but to make memory itself less of a personal burden, and to contain distractions at their root by externalizing what so often slips the mind, and by actively managing the daily flow-breakers unique to a busy household.

This chapter addresses the practical side of ADHD time struggles: moving memory and focus out of one's head and into the physical world, using targeted supports. Each tool and process described below is designed to bolster the routines from the previous chapter, reduce avoidable stress, and make forgetfulness or distraction feel less like a personal flaw and more like a solvable friction point.

## Tools Checklist: Tactile, Digital, and Visual Supports

ADHD moms often benefit from bringing reminders and task prompts into their immediate environment. Rather than relying on willpower or mental lists, physical and digital aids cue action where and when it is needed most. These tools fall into three categories tactile, digital, and visual each serving a different function, depending on personal preference and household context.

***Tactile Supports:***

- **Sticky notes:** Use for immediate, high-priority reminders ("Lunchbox!" on the door). Color coding boosts their visibility.
- **Timers:** Employ kitchen timers or small battery units for tasks that tend to drift (laundry, screentime, transitions).
- **Token jars or checkboxes:** Track recurring chores or self-care actions. Moving a bead, stacking blocks for completed routines, or checking off small boxes provides instant feedback.
- **Clipboards or magnetic pads:** Attach to the fridge or central command area to list daily errands or repeated routines.

***Digital Supports:***

- **Smartphone reminders:** Program recurring alarms for key tasks (medications, pick-up times, permission slips).
- **Tracking apps:** Use family-shared apps like Google Keep, Todoist, or Cozi for collaborative lists with kids or partners.
- **Calendar alerts with vibrant icons:** Choose bright emoji-flagged notifications instead of plain text to catch the eye quickly.
- **Wearable tech:** If comfortable, smartwatches or simple vibrating wristbands can signal time to shift, stand, or wrap up.

***Visual Supports:***

- **Whiteboards:** Place in central areas (kitchen, hallway) for displaying the day's color blocks or urgent tasks.

- **Color charts:** Use color-coded cards or chart boards for categories of routines (purple for school admin tasks, green for play, etc).
- **Visual calendars:** Large paper calendars with stickers, icons, or drawings signal week-at-a-glance priorities helpful for both adults and kids.
- **Task checklists with pictures:** Particularly useful for routines involving children, as well as for moms who think visually.

Mixing these supports is sometimes necessary. An ADHD home may thrive on sticky notes plus a whiteboard in the kitchen, digital reminders for outside-the-house anchors, and a visible timer for transitional routines. Moms can audit which types of cues work best for their attention style and focus tool usage where forgetfulness or distraction clusters.

After assembling the right tools, the next level is to structure where memory gets externalized within the home environment.

## Identifying an "External Memory Spot" in Each Room

One frequent challenge is losing track of reminders because household clutter or chaos hides them. Instead of adding more reminders everywhere, effective externalization depends on creating a consistent "memory spot" in each major space. This is a pre-designated, visible area where urgent tasks, notes, or cues can always be found, reducing the mental scramble of searching for reminders.

***Steps to establish and maintain an external memory spot:***

- Identify the rooms most commonly used during busy periods (kitchen, entryway, living room, bathroom).
- Choose a small section in each room, ideally at eye level and near a habitual pause point (by the door, above a counter, next to the light switch).
- Designate the area with a distinctive visual cue colored tape border, a mini whiteboard, or a magnetic strip.
- Place only essential reminders or objects in this spot. For example, the kitchen might have the day's dinner plan; the entryway displays a sticky note checklist of what to grab before exiting.
- Clean and replenish the memory spot daily, tossing irrelevant notes and adding the next priority item.

By standardizing the location and purpose of these external memory spots, it becomes automatic to check them before moving on. Over time, family members can be looped in, so reminders are not hidden or misplaced by others, but remain accessible and visible for communal needs.

Once these physical memory anchors are in place, attention shifts to understanding the "why" and "when" behind everyday interruptions.

## Daily Distraction Diagnostic: Mapping Interruption Sources

Distractions multiply in ADHD homes, often adding to time losses in unpredictable ways. Instead of treating all interruptions as equal, it is useful to map where, when, and how often disruptions occur and whether they stem from environment, people, technology, or internal cues (like shifting energy).

A daily distraction diagnostic form can clarify which parts of the day and which types of tasks are most vulnerable to interruption. Completing this form for several days provides actionable data, not just a vague sense of overwhelm.

**Sample distraction diagnostic form:**

**Time of day:**

**Task/activity in progress:**

**Interruption type (check all that apply):**

- Child asks for hclp
- Phone or device notification
- Environmental (noise, pet, doorbell)
- Mind wandering/thought chain
- Incoming call/message
- Sudden emotional urge (snack, social media, etc)Was the interruption avoidable? (Y/N)How did you respond? (A) Ignored, (B) Switched focus, (C) Lost track, (D) Delayed main taskImpact on task: (A) None, (B) Minor delay, (C) Major disruption, (D) Abandoned

Filling out even a brief checklist like this can reveal patterns. For example, if phone notifications and child requests cluster around meal prep, that window becomes a priority for protection—perhaps by muting devices or instituting a short "do not disturb" kitchen period.

This exercise also distinguishes between unavoidable interruptions (urgent child needs, emergencies) and those subject to environmental tweaks or habit changes. Awareness cuts down on unfair self-blame and directs problem-solving to concrete elements.

Establishing what truly requires memory effort, and what can be delegated to external tools, is the next practical filter.

## Priority Filter: Remember, Write, or Release

Not everything needs to be remembered or managed personally each day. Moms with ADHD often feel pressured to capture every detail, piling on both cognitive load and unnecessary systems. Instead, a simple three-part filter can help decide what deserves mental space, what belongs on a list or reminder, and what is safe to skip.

***Priority filter for daily memory tasks:***

1. **Critical to remember (no externalization):**

   Only non-deferrable, high-stakes items that cannot be missed without real consequence. Examples: picking up a child at a set time, medication doses, critical appointments.

2. **Write down or externalize:**

Tasks, appointments, or ideas that will not cause acute problems if delayed, but could create stress if forgotten. Examples: meal planning, administrative forms, household supply lists, calls to return, school emails. These go onto whiteboards, lists, sticky notes, or app reminders in designated memory spots.

3. **Safe to release—not tracked:**

   Low-impact chores, thoughts, or "shoulds" that do not require attention today. Examples might include optional home organizing, random errands, or social media updates. Letting go of these, at least on a given day, is not neglect but a conscious act of cognitive triage.

Applying this filter helps limit the "all-or-nothing" tendencies of ADHD overwhelm. Moms can calibrate memory strategies for what actually serves their current priorities, reducing both tool fatigue and emotional guilt.

To tie it all together, reminders and support work best when they are seamlessly connected to the routine flow and environment, a foundation step for true follow-through.

## Linking Reminders to Environmental Cues

For reminders to drive action (instead of being part of the scenery), they must be linked to strong environmental cues. These cues are physical locations, routine events, or sensory triggers that make the reminder visible or noticeable exactly when needed, transforming intention into follow-through.

*Framework for linking reminders:*

- **Place visual cues exactly where the action occurs.** For example, stick a "grab lunch!" note on the fridge handle, not the counter. Position a timer at the workstation, not in the drawer.
- **Use "anchored routines"—pair a reminder with an existing habit.** For instance, leave evening medication next to the toothbrush, or place school forms on top of the lunch box that is opened every morning.
- **Reinforce with multi-sensory cues.** Combine a visual with an auditory (a checklist by the door and a chime at the relevant time), or a tactile with a visual (move a clothespin along a string to depict finished tasks).
- **Rotate cues to prevent habituation flatness.** Change sticky note colors every week, or swap which cupboard receives the "critical" reminder, so the signal remains fresh and eye-catching.
- **Involve family in cue-response rituals.** Ask a child to check the entryway memory spot before leaving, or a partner to confirm calendar appointments after dinner.

The key principle is that reminders and supports should not exist in a vacuum. Instead, their placement and design anticipate daily traffic, natural pauses, and points of recurring forgetfulness. Environmental linkage turns reminders into trusted supports rather than background noise.

Adopting these tools, spots, diagnostics, filters, and integrated reminders shifts the burden of remembering and resisting distractions from internal grit to practical structure. Externalizing memory and managing distractions in an ADHD mom's world is not a luxury but an essential act of self-support. This approach sets the stage for reducing micro-failures and creating space for smoother daily flow allowing mothers to focus energy where it matters most, not on battling invisible friction. If ongoing struggles with memory or distractions significantly disrupt functioning or well-being, consider revisiting the earlier safety note and consulting a qualified professional for deeper guidance.

# Micro-Transitions and Buffer Zones: Reducing the Cost of Shifts

Daily life in an ADHD household rarely flows in a straight line. As you refine your Time Code system, you may find that even with visual reminders and memory aids everywhere, stumbling blocks still appear most often during transitions. Shifting from one activity to another especially when kids, chores, and personal needs all collide poses challenges that go beyond simple forgetfulness. This is where micro-transitions and intentional buffer zones come in, making the movement between daily anchors not only possible, but smoother and less costly in stress or lost time.

Rather than striving to run the day on strict schedules, ADHD moms thrive with spacious, flexible shifts. The following tools and guides are built to support each movement point in your routine, carving out room to breathe, reset, and regain focus before the next demand takes over. This chapter gives you hands-on frameworks not just reminders that cushion those moments and lower the hidden "tax" of constantly switching gears.

## Template for Building Strategic Buffer Zones

Transitions don't just "happen." For moms juggling multiple roles and demands, even minor activity changes can trigger lags, emotional friction, or spirals of distraction. Strategic buffer zones—deliberate, short windows between major daily events cushion the impact of each jump and turn a rushed scramble into a manageable glide.

Here's a practical template for building five- to fifteen-minute buffer zones into your day's natural movement points:

1. **Identify your four or five highest-friction transitions. Typical candidates:**
    - Getting kids out the door in the morning
    - Returning from errands or school run
    - Transitioning from work to family/home duties
    - Preparing for bed or winding down
2. **For each, look at the earliest realistic end time** of the prior activity, and the latest tolerable start time for the next. Build in a 5–15 minute zone between. If schedules overlap tightly, even five minutes of grace is worth adding.
3. **Mark these buffer windows on your existing Color Block or Time Code chart.** Visually differentiate them with a unique color, doodle, or symbol associated with "pause" (such as a circle or a coffee cup).
4. **In each buffer, define only one objective:** to pause, reset, and prep for the next step, not to sneak in more chores. Use this time to check reminders, gather belongings, or simply breathe.
5. **Make family members aware of buffer zones** by giving them a shared name ("soft start," "switch spot," or "reset minute"). Let kids know these are mini-wait zones, and help them understand not everything has to change at once.

Even small nudges like this can dramatically reduce lateness, friction, and forgotten items. If you repeatedly miss buffer time, review the transition points, is the previous block consistently too long, or does the next event need more realistic timing? Adjust buffer placement every few weeks based on daily patterns.

Moving into the next section, mastering the shift from one activity to another isn't just about the moments in between, but about how you move from one to the next. Rituals serve as on-ramps and off-ramps, making it easier for both mom and kids to begin and end activities smoothly.

## "Starter Rituals" Checklist for Smooth Activity Changes

ADHD brains often resist abrupt stopping or starting. Rituals, even ultra-simple ones can prime minds and bodies for a shift. When used regularly, these small actions signal that it's time to wind down, gear up, or switch context. Effective rituals don't require elaborate routines; they just need to be predictable and repeatable.

***Here's a starter checklist for choosing and setting up smooth transition rituals:***

1. **For Starting a New Activity:**
   - Play a designated "start" song or chime
   - Do a quick physical stretch or shakeout
   - State aloud, "We're switching to [activity] now."
   - Gather the key object(s) for the next event (bag, water bottle, book)
   - Set a timer if the following task is time-bound
2. **For Ending an Activity:**

- Use a gentle "wind-down" phrase ("Let's finish up and get ready to switch.")
- Put away key items together as a closing act
- Turn off environmental cues from the prior activity (music, screens, lights)
- Give a 2-minute warning, especially for younger kids ("You have 2 minutes left with [activity].")
- Celebrate completion with a small gesture (high five, silly dance, sticker)

3. **For High-Stress Transitions:**
   - Take 3 slow breaths together
   - Validate any resistance or emotions ("It's hard to stop when you're having fun.")
   - Offer a micro-choice ("Do you want to carry your shoes or your snack to the car?")

Consider printing or writing this checklist as a "ritual card" posted near your highest-friction points (front door, bathroom, bedside). Use rituals consistently at the same points each day so they become reliable cues, not extra chores for you to remember.

Now that you've set up transition cushions and rituals, it's worth clarifying why some shifts still drag, even with good intentions in place. Some barriers are uniquely ADHD-driven; others are simply the stuff of family life.

## Flow Blockers Identification Grid

Not all transition slowdowns have the same source. Differentiating ADHD-specific inertia from routine parenting friction empowers you to tailor strategies, rather than blaming yourself or applying the wrong fix.

***Here is a flow blockers identification grid to help spot the difference:***

- If the delay involves feeling "stuck," knowing you need to get moving but unable to break the current activity's pull likely ADHD inertia.
- If moving to a new activity includes overwhelming the number of steps (change clothes, gather bags, prep snacks) likely ADHD-related step paralysis.
- If the blockage comes from kid resistance, bathroom needs, snack debates, or last-minute forgotten items it's a typical parenting slowdown.
- If your mind "falls blank" on what comes next, with a sense of internal fuzziness or time-drift ADHD-based transition slip.
- If a slow-down is caused by external events (unexpected visitor, lost shoe, fight between siblings) general family-life disruption.

Using the grid, mark each real transition pause you encounter this week. Note the type and source: is this mainly an ADHD friction or a shared family event? This clarity helps you choose supports: more reminders or rituals for ADHD inertia, direct help for kid chaos, or contingency plans for genuine surprises.

Once you've separated the types of slowdowns, the next step involves practical strategies to self-regulate especially when a "bad shift" looms or routines unravel.

## Cheat Sheet: Mini Self-Regulation Strategies at Common Trouble Spots

ADHD-friendly self-regulation does not rely on sheer willpower, but rather quick access to calming and activating tactics tailored to known trouble points. Use this cheat sheet at typical friction moments:

**Leaving the House:**

- Use a "staging area" for bags, coats, keys (set out the night before if possible)
- Set a repeating alarm or doorframe sticky note as a "now is the time" cue
- Group needed items in a clear tote or by the doorway
- Designate a 2-minute "check and reset" before leaving; breathe, scan, go

**Bedtime and Wind Down:**

- Start dimming lights 30 minutes before desired bedtime
- Place a visual checklist near the bathroom or bedroom door: pajamas, brush teeth, water cup
- Use a specific bedtime scent (lotion, pillow spray) to cue winding down
- For kids: offer a small incentive for each completed bedtime step (sticker, story)

**Transitioning from Work/School to Home:**

- Change into "at home" clothing to signal activity shift
- Spend 5 quiet minutes with a drink or snack as a decompression buffer

- Review a whiteboard or note for evening priorities only the next 1–2 tasks
- Allow yourself (and kids) one "filler" activity (favorite show, solo play) before jumping into demands

**Errands/Outings:**

- Prepare a "go bag" the night before (snacks, wipes, entertainment)
- Review the list out loud with kids or yourself before leaving
- Accept that not every errand will get done: circle the top 1–2 priorities to keep focus sharp

Place this cheat sheet where you can grab it fast. If the first option fails, try a backup. The point is to have a menu of actions, not to depend on memory at stressful moments.

## Early Warning Checklist: Are You Rushing or Running Behind?

ADHD time blindness can hide the signs of an impending rush until the pressure is overwhelming. Early detection, along with reset actions, can pull you back to center before stress snowballs. Use this early warning checklist:

- Are you skipping usual steps (no breakfast, no checklist, left stuff behind)?
- Do you feel your heart rate rising or hands getting tense?
- Are you snapping at kids or yourself, or using harsh self-talk?
- Are you forgetting where you put something you just had?
- Have you stopped pausing for breath, water, or personal needs?

***If you notice two or more of these signals:***

**Reset steps:**

- Pause. Physically stop for ten to thirty seconds, even if it feels impossible.
- Take three slow breaths. Count each exhale.
- Name the next single task, aloud if possible.
- If late is inevitable, message or call the relevant party (school, sitter) if practical.
- Let go of guilt for pausing; remind yourself that a short reset saves more time than it loses long term.

Regular use of this checklist and reset protocol can convert panicked rushing into a chance to regain your own pace and protect your energy. Share the signals with partners or older kids so everyone can help each other spot the signs and participate in the rescue.

Each of these tools, buffer zones, rituals, flow identification, regulation, and early resets fits directly into the unique realities of ADHD motherhood. Used together, they shift your day from relentless scramble toward something more measured, predictable, and forgiving.

This approach does not eliminate chaos, but it does reduce its sting. With these frameworks, you create breathing room inside the most challenging parts of your day, making each transition feel a little less sharp, and a lot more manageable.

# Emotional First Aid for Bad Time Days

The unpredictability of an ADHD day rarely stops with just logistical snafus. Once routines go off course buffer zones missed, reminders ignored, transitions fumbled the resulting emotions often take center stage. Feelings of panic, frustration, or shame can sweep through fast, sometimes even before the practical aftermath is fully clear. This is when emotional first aid becomes just as essential as time management. Rather than waiting for a whole day (or week) to unravel, the right self-regulation tools can soften these difficult moments and create a path back to stability.

Where previous chapters focused on external routines and physical supports, this chapter turns to the emotional toolkit: frameworks and scripts for managing the mental toll of "bad time days." The goal is to handle those inevitable setbacks with compassion, clarity, and restore inner balance while actively blocking shame spirals and the weight of outside expectations.

## The Four-Level Emotional Regulation Ladder for Time-Related Overwhelm

Managing the emotional fallout of a missed deadline, forgotten appointment, or a morning lost to distractions requires a stepwise approach. The Four-Level Emotional Regulation Ladder is designed specifically for ADHD moms facing time-related overwhelm. It offers concrete actions for each escalation point helping shift from panic back to problem-solving.

1. **Level One: Body Check-In**

   Pause and ask, "What do I feel physically right now?" This step grounds awareness in the body (racing heart, clenched jaw, shallow breath) rather than getting swept away by self-recriminations. Adjust posture, unclench fists, or take a sip of water.

2. **Level Two: Emotional Label**

   Identify and name the emotion: Is this panic? Frustration? Shame? Saying it aloud or writing it down interrupts the unhelpful cycle and makes the feeling less overwhelming.

3. **Level Three: Context Reframe**

   Remind yourself of context: "I have ADHD, and my brain processes time differently." This is not a personal failing, but an expected feature of the ADHD experience. Acknowledge any external factors that contributed to child illness, surprise errands, unexpected demands.

4. **Level Four: Next Micro-Action**

   Look for the smallest next step that could help, such as texting to apologize, moving one thing from to-do to "done," or simply resetting the plan for the next hour. This step breaks the freeze response and nudges momentum forward.

When the entire ladder feels out of reach (for example, during full-blown panic), focus only on the first rung body check-in. Even a small physical reset can interrupt escalation and buy time for further recovery.

## Emergency Script Card Set for Moments of Panic, Shame, or Frustration

Verbalizing calming words during intense eruptions of emotion can be challenging. Having a set of prepared, repeatable scripts acts as a lifeline during sudden surges of anxiety or guilt. These Emergency Script Cards are short, concrete phrases designed for the immediate aftermath of time loss or disruption:

***Emergency Script Card Set:***

- "This is a hard moment, not a forever problem."
- "My brain works differently, and that's allowed."
- "It's okay to start again right now."
- "Mistakes are data, not disasters."
- "I can only do one next thing."
- "Guilt is a feeling, not a fact."
- "I deserve kindness, even on difficult days."

Keep these scripts on sticky notes, a phone wallpaper, or a notecard in a purse or planner. Use them as anchors anytime ruminations or self-blame begin to take over. While these phrases might feel "small," they serve as powerful pattern-interrupts, especially when consistently repeated.

The internal transition here is from emotional resetting to defending against external pressures and advice that can reinforce shame or overwhelm.

## Rule Set for Identifying Toxic Productivity Advice and Setting Boundaries

Much of the public advice around productivity and time management does not align with ADHD realities or worse, directly undermines the process of compassionate self-regulation. Learning to spot and filter out harmful messaging is key to emotional first aid.

***Rule Set for Spotting Toxic Productivity Advice:***

- If it presents a single failure (missed task) as a sign of moral weakness or laziness, discard it.
- If advice assumes flawless memory, attention, or energy every day, treat it as incompatible.
- If it insists on rigid hourly schedules with zero margin, recognize it fails to account for ADHD's fluctuating focus.
- If shaming, fear, or threats are used as motivators, exclude it from your circle.
- If it triggers guilt for prioritizing rest, play, or recovery, challenge or avoid it.

***Setting Boundaries with Others:***

- **Respond calmly but firmly:** "Those methods don't work with my brain. I follow an ADHD-friendly routine."
- **Offer an alternative:** "What supports me is flexibility and visual cues—not rigid checklists."
- **Refuse guilt:** "I'm learning to focus on progress, not perfection."

When criticism or "helpful" advice slips in from family, friends, or colleagues, it helps to have a prepared script: "I'm working with a time system designed for my ADHD. Thanks, but I'm using what works for me." Consistently enforcing these boundaries protects emotional wellbeing and strengthens self-respect.

Shifting from public perception to personal communication, the next focus is on handling post-disruption conversations with family.

## Memo Template for Communicating Needs to Family After a Day of Time Losses

After a day of missed pickups, dropped chores, or forgotten events, the urge to withdraw or self-criticize may be strong. Instead, clear and concise communication with family can prevent misunderstandings and foster support. Use this memo template to express needs without inviting blame.

**Family Needs Memo Template (fill-in blanks as appropriate):**

***Subject: Today Was a Tough Time Day***

Hi [Family Member(s)],

Today was one of those days when my sense of time got away from me. If I seemed rushed, distracted, or missed something, it wasn't deliberate. My brain handles time differently, and sometimes things slip—especially on hectic days.

What would help me right now is [space, a reset moment, help with one chore, gentle reminders, understanding]. I want you to know I'm working on it (with my ADHD Time Code system), and your support matters. If you have questions or want to talk about how we can do things differently next time, I'm open as soon as I'm settled.

Thanks for your patience and for being a team with me.

Love,[Your Name]

Send or read this memo when you need extra understanding. It doesn't apologize for ADHD but reaffirms effort, names support needs, and keeps family channels open. Open conversations are essential, yet there are situations when self-support falls short and seeking additional help is the wise choice.

## Early Signal Checklist for When Professional or Peer Support Is Advisable

Not every bad time day can or should be navigated solo. Identifying when patterns shift from manageable to unmanageable can prevent crises and keep emotional struggles from deepening. **Use this checklist to recognize when to reach beyond the home toolkit:**

- Repeated time losses (more than three times per week) are causing family or work distress that feels unfixable.
- Intense feelings of shame, sadness, or anger linger for days or disrupt sleep.
- Withdrawal from loved ones increases; conversations about time struggles become rare or tense.
- Coping scripts and regulation ladders no longer interrupt rumination or panic.
- Thoughts of being "unfit" or "beyond help" recur, especially at the start of the day.

- Relying on quick fixes (food, screens, snapping at kids) grows more frequent.
- No sense of hope or progress, even when trying new tools or strategies.

***If two or more signals appear in a single week, consider reaching out to:***

- A mental health professional specializing in ADHD, family support, or stress
- Peer support groups (local, online ADHD mom groups, or general parenting groups)
- A trusted friend or partner who offers nonjudgmental listening

Early outreach reduces the chance of becoming isolated or entrenched in shame. The safety note from earlier chapters applies: seeking support is a strength, not a failure, and community or professional input often unlocks new, sustainable solutions.

With all of these resources, the ultimate aim is for each mom to move through even her hardest time days without getting stuck. Emotional first aid is not about bypassing feelings, but meeting them directly, working through them in manageable steps, and protecting self-worth in every stage.

Together, these tools, the regulation ladder, script cards, boundary rules, needs memo, and early signal checklist serve as a shield and a reset button. While external routines can be rebuilt and plans rescheduled, the emotional waves of ADHD time blindness can be softened and reshaped with practice. Each skill becomes a small act of kindness directed inward, creating space for growth, grace, and more gentle days ahead.

# Consistency, Accountability, and Rebound Tools

Every attempt at emotional regulation, no matter how steady, will eventually bump into the brick wall of real life. Good intentions and self-compassionate scripts help soften chaotic moments, but mothers living with ADHD often find that managing feelings is only half the equation. Progress is often blocked by the challenge of repeating routines, maintaining follow-through, or "rebounding" after everything collapses. This chapter directly addresses those gaps: providing accessible accountability, realistic ways to measure progress, and tools that make it possible to recover quickly after setbacks without the hidden trap of shame.

Having explored how to regulate reactions when plans fail, the focus now shifts to staying on track and regaining calm after routines are disrupted. Sustained consistency, paired with the right support systems, forms a unique safety net for ADHD moms determined to build new habits that work with their brains—not against them.

## Gentle Accountability Options

Traditional accountability models praise relentless follow-up and strict checking. While these might work for some, many ADHD moms experience them as pressure-cookers, triggering defensiveness or avoidance instead of motivation. Instead, low-pressure, gentle systems make it easier to keep commitments without compounding guilt. Three options stand out for daily life:

1. **Text Buddies:** A text buddy is a trusted friend, often another mom or a partner who agrees to exchange short, supportive messages about the day's main goal, trouble spot, or upcoming routine. The goal is not to enforce compliance, but to offer a moment of shared attention. For example: "Starting laundry now ping me in 20 if you remember!" or "Did you get to pause yet today?"
2. **Visual Trackers:** Many mothers with ADHD respond well to visible reminders of progress. Visual trackers include habit charts on the fridge, magnetic boards, sticker calendars, or a sheet of colored circles that get filled in for each routine maintained. The key is to keep tracking simple and quick, not another time-draining task. The act of placing a sticker, crossing a box, or moving a token can serve as a tiny, tangible reward.
3. **Audible Prompts:** Alarms, chime reminders, or voice notes recorded on a phone create external nudges at critical times. Unlike scheduled calendars that risk being ignored, setting unique sounds for different activities or choosing a "song cue" for each daily anchor (like a morning playlist) gives cross-sensory support. The prompt nudges the mind back to the routine with minimal effort.

Each of these options can be customized. Some moms use all three for different routines, while others select whichever matches energy and mental bandwidth that week. The aim is never perfection, but to build an environment that gently reminds rather than scolds.

## Template for Setting Reset Points

One common trap for ADHD moms is the "all-or-nothing" mentality: the idea that if a routine is interrupted or missed, the only answer is to start completely over. This thinking leads to wasted energy and deepened discouragement. Instead, introducing "reset points" helps reframe every disruption as a regular part of progress.

***To set a reset point, use this simple template each time a routine is derailed:***

1. **Name the Routine:** (Example: Morning kid drop-off prep)
2. **Describe What Happened:** (What disrupted or halted the process? Did someone get sick? Was there a forgotten item? Did time slip away due to distraction?)
3. **Set a Nearby Restart:** (Identify the next safe, realistic moment for resuming. "After breakfast," "when kids are packed up," or "as soon as I locate keys." Avoid waiting for the next day or a "clean slate.")
4. **Tiny Adjustment:** (What one tweak could make a re-entry easier? Postpone a less urgent task, prep items the night before, or change the sequence slightly.)
5. **Self-Kind Check:** (Briefly note one thing done well "I caught myself before major meltdown," "I asked for help" to cement a non-shaming narrative.)

**Reset Point Template**

- Today's Routine: ____________
- What shifted/disrupted it: ____________
- Fastest next moment to reset: ____________

- One easy change to try: ____________
- What I handled well (no matter how small): ____________

Completing this reset template takes less than two minutes and can be done on paper, phone, or in your mind. Doing so allows routines to "bend" instead of break, cutting recovery time and protecting self-worth.

## Flexible Routine Tracker: Logging Without Shame

Routine tracking traditionally relies on the idea of streaks—unbroken chains of days. That model often fails for those with ADHD-related time perception difficulties. Instead, use a flexible tracker designed to record both when a routine is followed and when disruptions happen, but without penalty, erasure, or blame.

***Flexible Routine Tracker Design***

- List your chosen routines along the left side of a grid (bedtime, dishes, 10-minute tidy-up, evening prep).
- Along the top, set dates or days of the week.
- Each day, mark routines in one of three ways: completed (circle or star), disrupted (neutral dash or different color), or reset (arrow icon, showing a bounced-back effort later in the day).
- Write a brief note under major disruptions if desired: "School project," "sick kid," "lost track after phone call."
- Review the grid each Sunday. Count how many resets (not just "successes") were logged.

Why this method works: ADHD time blindness often erases memories of partial or adapted successes. Blending streaks and disruptions in one place highlights resilience rather than just slips. The presence of resets on the chart reinforces that progress is nonlinear and rewards repeated starts—not supposed one-and-done discipline.

This type of routine log can be marked on printable trackers, dry-erase boards, or an app that allows for custom icons. The emphasis should always be on reflection, not self-critique.

## Low-Pressure vs. High-Pressure Accountability Tools

Choosing the right style of accountability can mean the difference between new habits sticking or causing avoidance. The comparison below outlines common ADHD-mom responses to different accountability environments.

***Low-Pressure Accountability***

- **Examples:** text buddies, visual trackers, gentle alarms, collaborative logs
- **Description:** Supports routines with reminders, encouragement, or tracking; does not involve negative consequences for slips
- **Best for:** Building confidence, treating routines as experiments, protecting motivation
- **Common responses:** Relief, willingness to try again, less fear of failure

***High-Pressure Accountability***

- **Examples:** formal coaching contracts, public goal declarations, strict checklists, penalties for uncompleted tasks
- **Description:** Imposes external obligations with consequences for non-compliance; aims to "enforce" behavior
- **Best for:** Short, urgent deadlines where external stakes prompt action (rarely sustainable for ADHD-mom daily life)
- **Common responses:** Anxiety, resistance, guilt spirals, rapid drop-out rates

Aim to choose or adapt accountability methods toward the low-pressure side. When faced with a necessary high-pressure demand (such as a critical deadline), pair it with backup prompts, more frequent resets, or a visual routine log to prevent spirals. Most daily routines benefit from tools that offer room for error—and celebrate repeated attempts.

## Three Common Failure Modes for ADHD Accountability (and How to Recover)

Even with the right tools, most ADHD moms will recognize three persistent failure modes when trying to maintain accountability:

1. **The "Shame Shutdown"**

   **Symptoms:** Skipping check-ins, hiding routine logs, or abandoning the process after a mistake, driven by embarrassment or internal criticism.

   **Recovery:**

   - Pause and name the emotional trigger without judgment.

- Use the reset template to reclaim a sense of agency: "Disruption happened, and here's my fast re-entry."
- Ask a text buddy for a no-judgment check-in. Normalize talking about slips, not just successes.

2. **The "Tool Overload"**

   Symptoms: Chasing the perfect system, downloading multiple apps, using too many logs or reminders at once, leading to confusion and dropping all tools in frustration.

   **Recovery:**

   - Choose a single tracker or buddy system for a week. Commit to ignoring other tools until a natural rhythm emerges.
   - If overwhelmed, switch to purely analog cues (sticky notes or visual boards).
   - Remind yourself that "more" is rarely better. ADHD brains thrive with less internal clutter.

3. **The "Invisible Progress Trap"**

   Symptoms: Overlooking or discounting partial efforts, thinking only "full compliance" counts as success, leading to underappreciation of actual gains (such as partial resets, micro-routines, or adapting routines midstream).

   **Recovery:**

   - Revisit the flexible routine tracker and highlight every logged reset or modification.

- Conduct a five-minute weekly recap: What partial wins occurred? Which start-overs, even if late, kept the chain moving?
- Enlist an accountability partner to "spotlight" small improvements that might otherwise go unnoticed.

Layering these recovery actions on top of the consistency tools builds a resilient routine ecology. Each time a system wobbles or fails, the ability to self-correct using resets, simplification, or reframed progress is a greater indicator of success than any single, unbroken run.

The ADHD Mom's Time Code is not about achieving perfect consistency, or never veering off course, but about developing practical rhythms of return. With gentle accountability systems, clear reset practices, and trackers that honor effort over results, ADHD moms gain realistic structures for managing daily routines—without extra layers of blame. Every reset and every comeback becomes an act of progress and persistence. These tools not only support external habits, but reinforce an internal trust: time can be lost and reclaimed, and consistency can be redefined one flexible step at a time.

# Building a Self-Compassionate Time Identity

Every routine and system in The ADHD Mom's Time Code supports one deeper goal: helping mothers with ADHD feel whole and worthy, even when time goes awry. While gentle accountability and flexible resets build needed structure, self-kindness is the essential anchor for lasting change. Progress in this framework is not about perfection or constant self-improvement; it thrives when moms form an identity grounded in self-forgiveness, the recognition of hidden wins, and compassionate adaptation to reality.

Cultivating a self-compassionate time identity begins with changing the way missteps and successes are seen. Time slippage is almost inevitable for many mothers with ADHD. Without self-acceptance, each mistake can revive old narratives of failure. This chapter outlines key practices daily, weekly, and in-the-moment to foster a resilient, kind relationship with time and oneself.

## Core checklist for practicing self-forgiveness when time slips occur

Losing track of time, missing appointments, or forgetting tasks often triggers a harsh inner critic. Real self-forgiveness is practical, not merely positive thinking. Use this checklist whenever plans fall apart or time escapes:

1. Acknowledge the slip directly ("I was late," "I forgot").

2. Pause activity for one minute to reduce the emotional charge: sit, stand still, or lean against a counter.
3. Name one external factor that contributed (interruptions, child needs, fatigue), even if others might "handle it." Externalizing cuts self-blame.
4. Make a neutral observation: "My brain lost the time flow. This is a neurological pattern, not a character flaw."
5. Use self-talk as you would with a friend: "You're allowed to try again. This does not erase past successes."
6. If repair is needed (apologizing, rescheduling), do it simply and move on.
7. Ask, "What's the smallest adjustment that could help if this happens again?" Note it with no pressure to master it now.

Following this checklist retrains knee-jerk responses, breaking the old spiral of guilt and rumination. Over time, these steps shape a mom's time identity into one that is flexible, realistic, and resilient.

Moving beyond forgiveness, long-term motivation depends on recognizing invisible efforts and valuing everyday solutions.

## Framework for celebrating invisible wins: adapting, pivoting, and outsourcing

Invisible wins are the small, essential actions that rarely get attention but keep life moving for ADHD moms: adjusting on the fly, shifting plans calmly, or asking for help rather than pushing through. Seeing these quiet victories strengthens self-esteem and shifts self-perception from failing to resourceful.

***Use this framework to celebrate invisible wins:***

1. At day's end, list one time you adapted a plan changed, a partial solution accepted, a task handed off, or a makeshift fix applied.
2. Once a week, write down or say a "pivot moment" that prevented a situation from worsening—like picking up takeout, editing a routine, or improvising childcare.
3. Keep an "outsource log." Every time a task is given to someone else, record it as a positive move, not a failure.
4. When discouraged, look back at these lists or recall past adaptations. Highlight these as creative solutions.
5. Share a favorite adaptation with another ADHD mom to support community recognition of hidden labor.

By consistently recognizing these invisible wins, ADHD moms can build confidence and celebrate their unique strengths. Over time, this practice helps shift focus from perceived shortcomings to daily resourcefulness. Remember, every small adaptation is a testament to creativity and resilience. Sharing these victories not only honors your efforts but also strengthens the community of support.

## Affirmation card set: daily encouragement for ADHD-mom challenges

Effective self-talk must be specific and believable for ADHD moms. The following affirmation cards can be handwritten, printed, or added to phones as reminders. **These cards speak directly to common struggles:**

- "I am not behind, I am moving at my own pace, with the resources I have today."
- "Partial progress is worthy of celebration."
- "When time slips, I reset gently. Small restarts count."
- "Getting help is a smart time strategy, not a sign of weakness."
- "Adaptation is my superpower and my family benefits when I improvise."
- "Interruptions don't erase my intentions; I can pick up where I left off."
- "My worth is unchanged by any to-do list."
- "Invisible labor is still real labor, and I honor it."

Use these affirmations deliberately. Place them on mirrors, set as phone alerts, or read one before each challenging routine. Shuffle through them weekly to match the season's needs. Regular repetition builds more supportive thinking patterns.

Visible, recurring rituals further reinforce self-kindness and provide anchors for noticing growth or resetting after setbacks.

## Rituals for recognizing progress and resetting self-talk

Recognition rituals are structured pauses to appreciate small improvements. Their value lies in noticing incremental change, not achieving streaks.

***Progress recognition rituals include:***

- **Progress Jar:** Each day or week, write one flexible or accomplished act on a slip of paper to place in a jar or box. Over time, this collection gives visual evidence of growth.
- **Mirror Statements:** During daily routines like brushing teeth, look in the mirror and acknowledge one intentional act, no matter the outcome.
- **Weekly Reset Walk:** Take a short walk, mentally releasing shame about missed routines, then identify one tiny goal for the next week.
- **Five-Minute Celebration Pause:** Once a week, stop and list three adaptations made since Monday, speaking or writing them down.

***Self-talk reset rituals help after time slips:***

- **"Let It Go" Gesture:** Shake out your wrists, sigh, or close your notebook as a conscious signal to reset after a mistake.
- **Gentle Touch-Anchor:** Place a hand on your chest when self-judgment arises, repeating a phrase like, "Paused, not punished."
- **Intentional Message Swap:** Write down negative self-talk, then immediately rewrite it as a kind response.

Practicing these rituals helps ADHD moms replace old cycles of self-blame with regular opportunities for renewal and growth. Even with these tools, it's vital to watch for signs that perfectionism or chronic guilt is creeping back in.

## Red flag signals of perfectionism or chronic guilt and rapid interventions

Spotting red flags early allows for quick correction before shame overtakes momentum. Watch for these signals in yourself:

- Rigid, all-or-nothing rules return ("I must do this every day or not at all").
- Self-talk is harsh, with "always" and "never" attached to mistakes.
- Avoiding routines or trackers due to embarrassment.
- Dismissing all adaptations ("That didn't count because it wasn't planned.")
- Increased anxiety or irritability after missed routines.

***Respond quickly using these strategies:***

- **Secret Permission Slip:** Give explicit permission to start small, skip steps, or adapt. Write or say, "Today, good enough is enough."
- **Compassion Contact:** Message a peer, "I'm stuck in negativity—can you remind me of three things I adapted well this month?"
- **Micro-Reset:** Take two minutes to stretch, drink water, or step outside, reframing this as a new start.
- **Shame Disruption:** Name or write one recent success, no matter how small.
- **Perspective Pause:** Read an affirmation aloud, reminding yourself a missed routine does not define your week.

The sooner these interventions are applied, the easier it is to remain grounded in self-kindness and prevent old patterns from undermining self-worth.

Building a self-compassionate time identity is not a singular act but an ongoing process that deepens with practice. Each completed self-forgiveness checklist, celebrated adaptation, recited affirmation, and mindful ritual reconstructs the daily emotional foundation. Progress in The ADHD Mom's Time Code is not about flawless routines. It is found in recognizing and redirecting the return of harsh inner patterns before they take root.

By centering identity on resilience, creativity, and self-gentleness, ADHD moms gain confidence—even on days when plans unravel. The Time Code becomes more than a set of systems: it takes shape as an environment where self-respect, rather than perfection, sets the pace.

# Conclusion

With a self-compassionate time identity established, the process of managing time as an ADHD mom begins to shift from internal struggle to ongoing practice. Each tool and strategy introduced in The ADHD Mom's Time Code supports this core belief: your relationship with time is unique, and your worth does not depend on flawless routines or perfect days.

Looking back across the guide, you have added new structure and language to experiences that once felt confusing or isolating. Understanding your personal patterns of time blindness helped to explain missed appointments and persistent overwhelm, making space for curiosity instead of shame. Embracing the nonlinear nature of your days, you have learned to map energy levels, recognize invisible labor, and notice signals when routines start to unravel. The Guilt-Free Time Audit encouraged gentle awareness, showing how external pressures distort self-expectations and highlighting ways to reclaim priorities aligned with your real needs.

Transitions between these ideas built up a system the time code focused on flexibility instead of rigidity. Color blocks, anchor points, and adaptable scheduling all support your need for both structure and breathing room. The tools for memory and distraction management offer practical help, recognizing that externalizing reminders and cues often leads to more sustainable follow-through than endless mental effort. When extraction from routines is required, buffer zones and micro-transition rituals reduce the fallout, keeping daily flow from stalling or spiraling.

On hard days, the Emotional First Aid chapter gave practical ladders and scripts for handling overwhelm and pushing back on unrealistic productivity standards. The consistency and accountability tools acknowledge the episodic nature of ADHD motivation, offering a kinder definition of progress that factors in resets and streaks alike. Finally, the work of integrating daily self-forgiveness, celebrating invisible wins, and recognizing perfectionism as it returns cements an approach to time that honors the realities faced by mothers with ADHD.

What stands out across every chapter is the shift from a model of self-correction, heavy with guilt and external comparisons, to a model built on adaptation, external support, and self-respect. The ADHD Mom's Time Code does not guarantee that household or work life will run smoothly every day. Instead, it offers permission to experiment, reset, and recognize effort as you adapt routines to your evolving life context.

No system can erase the unpredictability of motherhood or the attentional challenges of ADHD. However, layering compassionate routines, concrete supports, and honest self-celebration brings a steadier foundation. Each adjustment, each external reminder, and every moment of self-kindness makes time less of an adversary and more of a partner in your daily life.

Carrying these strategies forward, remember that sustainable time management for ADHD moms happens incrementally. There will be slips, skipped routines, and occasional overwhelm. But now, equipped with the tools and frameworks here, you can meet these moments with perspective and self-kindness. Progress is measured not only by finished tasks but by each adaptation, reset, and the gradual, authentic claim to your own way of doing time.

You are not failing, you are managing complex realities with creativity, effort, and resilience. The ADHD Mom's Time Code belongs to you now. Use its framework as a guide, adjust boldly as needed, and trust that building a relationship with time anchored in honesty and compassion is not only possible, but profoundly valuable for yourself and your family.

# FAQs

**How do I start using the "time code" system if I hate routines?**

Many moms with ADHD find traditional routines too rigid or stifling, quickly falling apart in the face of real-life chaos. The "time code" system avoids this by using needs-based, flexible planning. Instead of strict schedules, you anchor broad color-coded zones around daily realities like school pickups or nap times that act as gentle guideposts.

To start, pick two anchors that almost always happen, such as breakfast or school pickup, and create color-coded time blocks around them. List the types of activities that typically fit into each block, like "morning swirl" (breakfast, teeth brushing, packing bags) or "afternoon swirl" (snack, homework, decompressing). Treat these as adaptable containers, not mandates, and add more blocks only as it feels natural. The goal is gentle predictability, not rigid structure.

**What's a realistic way to document lost time with a chaotic home life?**

Instead of detailed time logs, try "snapshot" documentation: quick, low-pressure daily check-ins. At day's end, jot down one block where time seemed to disappear, an unavoidable interruption (like a toddler meltdown), and a positive exception a moment that went better than expected. This helps you spot personal time drains, repeat triggers, and small wins. If writing is tough, use voice notes or photos as gentle reminders. The aim is awareness, not perfection.

**How do I explain my unique time management system to my partner or child's school?**

When explaining your approach, focus on shared goals keeping family life functional and reducing stress. Tell your partner you're using a color block system for structured flexibility, not strict schedules, and that support with anchor points (like reminders) helps ensure essentials happen.

For schools or caregivers, summarize: "We use a flexible routine based on big-picture anchors, not precise times, to support ADHD needs and family consistency." Be specific about what helps your family thrive.

**If digital reminders overwhelm me, are there low-tech alternatives?**

Absolutely. Many moms with ADHD prefer non-digital tools, which can be more effective. Try physical color-coded charts on the fridge, whiteboards with erasable lists, colored rubber bands as reminders, or kitchen timers for block transitions. Place visual cues in each room, like a basket of labeled cards or distinct mugs for morning and evening routines. These physical reminders often benefit kids as well.

**What if I slip back into old habits after a few weeks?**

Setbacks are normal, especially with ADHD. If you slip, pause and notice what changed. Revisit your anchors and color blocks. Do they still fit your reality? Restart with one micro-step, like resetting a single anchor or updating a reminder. Treat setbacks as neutral information and give yourself permission to adapt. The system is designed for rebounding, not perfection.

**Are these ADHD-friendly tools child-compatible?**

Most tools, especially visual and tactile supports, work well for kids—helping them anticipate transitions and participate in routines. Involve children in choosing anchor points and building routines together for more buy-in. Some elements, like personal affirmation cards, may be best kept as adult self-care.

**How can I seek outside help if my time struggles affect my mental health?**

If time management stress impacts your well-being, reaching out is a sign of strength. Start by talking with supportive friends or joining ADHD parent groups. For persistent challenges, consult an ADHD-informed mental health professional. Coaches or occupational therapists can also help. Bring your experiences with the time code system to professionals to guide next steps.

# References and Helpful Links

Ptacek, R., Weissenberger, S., Braaten, E. et al.. (2019). Clinical Implications of the Perception of Time in Attention Deficit Hyperactivity Disorder (ADHD): A Review. *Medical Science Monitor.* https://doi.org/10.12659/msm.914225

Sasaki, H., Jono, T., Fukuhara, R. et al.. (2022). Late-manifestation of attention-deficit/hyperactivity disorder in older adults: an observational study. *BMC Psychiatry.* https://doi.org/10.1186/s12888-022-03978-0

Brown, T.. "A New Understanding of ADHD in Children and Adults." https://doi.org/10.4324/9780203067536.

Hall, C., Taylor, J., Newell, K. et al.. (2016). The challenges of implementing ADHD clinical guidelines and research best evidence in routine clinical care settings: Delphi survey and mixed-methods study. *BJPsych Open.* https://doi.org/10.1192/bjpo.bp.115.002386

Mette, C.. (2023). Time Perception in Adult ADHD: Findings from a Decade—A Review. *International Journal of Environmental Research and Public Health.* https://doi.org/10.3390/ijerph20043098

Desrochers, B., Tuson, E., Magee, J.. (2019). Evaluation of Why Individuals with ADHD Struggle to Find Effective Digital Time Management Tools. *Proceedings of the 21st International ACM SIGACCESS Conference on Computers and Accessibility.* https://doi.org/10.1145/3308561.3354622

Wolraich, M., Hagan, J., Allan, C. et al.. (2019). Clinical Practice Guideline for the Diagnosis, Evaluation, and Treatment of Attention-Deficit/Hyperactivity Disorder in Children and Adolescents. *Pediatric Mental Health: A Compendium of AAP Clinical Practice Guidelines and Policies.* https://doi.org/10.1542/9781610023658-part01-clinical

Bussing, R., E Koro-Ljungberg, M., Williamson, P. et al.. (2006). What "Dr. Mom" ordered: A community-based exploratory study of parental self-care responses to children's ADHD symptoms. *Social Science & Medicine*. https://doi.org/10.1016/j.socscimed.2006.03.014

www.ingramcontent.com/pod-product-compliance
Lightning Source LLC
LaVergne TN
LVHW022016200926
848481LV00007B/2424